DISCOVER

LOURDES
In Bernadette's footsteps

Father Joseph BORDES

Translator English version : Father John LOCHRAN

Preface

The accounts in this booklet owe everything to the authoritative works of Father René Laurentin, Father Ravier (s.j.), and Dom Bernard Billet (O.S.B.). Those wishing a more comprehensive and more detailed account of Lourdes and Bernadette should refer to these works (see the Bibliography).

I was also aided in my meditation on the founding events of Lourdes by the books « Mary reveals Jesus to Bernadette », by Dom Eugène Vandeur (O.S.B.), and « The Symbolism of Lourdes » by Father Gasnier (O.P.).

I have written this booklet in response to the lively interest shown by pilgrims and by friends at Lourdes ; it was their constant demand for a popular work that forced me to put pen to paper. The simple account of those facts and events, words and gestures expressed and witnessed by Bernadette at the Grotto of Massabielle and during her lifetime, have always held tremendous appeal.

May these unforgettable images of Lourdes help the reader to say yes to the Message of Lourdes.

Father Joseph BORDES

Bibliography

R. Laurentin and D.B. Billet : *Authentic Accounts of Lourdes, The True Story - Bernadette speaks - Bernadette at home* (Published by Lethielleux)
R. Laurentin : The life of Bernadette (D.D. Brouwer)
P. Ravier : The writings of Saint Bernadette and her spiritual life (Lethielleux)
D.B. Billet : *Bernadette. An « everday » vocation* (Lethielleux)
Estrade : *Intimate memoires of a witness* (Published by Edit. Imp. de la Grotte)
Lasserre : *Notre-Dame de Lourdes* (1869)
Sempé-Duboé : *Notre-Dame de Lourdes* (Letourey et Ane 1931)
D.B. Billet et Pierre Lafourcade : *Pilgrim's guide to Lourdes* (D.D. Brouwer 1981).

« What good can come from Nazareth ? »

Such was the question put by Nathaniel, the future apostle, to his friend Phillip regarding a certain Jesus, the son of a carpenter who came from this unknown village in the Galilean countryside.

A similar question could have been asked about Lourdes in the year 1858. What good can come from Lourdes ? What made this little village with its 3,393 inhabitants any more special or any different from any other town or village anywhere else in the world ?

Lourdes was very proud of its magnificent Castle perched on a hilltop overlooking the town. But this old fortress which guarded the entrance to the mountain valleys was no more than a reminder of an inglorious and bloody past. It stood as a symbol of man's inhumanity to man, of that aggressive and domineering instinct which cause men to oscillate between violence and fear to the detriment of the poor and weak.

If Lourdes had a history, and certainly the great and famous had left their mark upon it, it was a history remembered more for its wars and battles than for anything else.

There was the legend of Mirat the Saracen chief who held the Castle against the assaults of Charlemagne. The coat of arms of Lourdes still bears witness to this legend of how Mirat sent Charlemagne a trout from a mountain stream as a sign that he could hold the Castle indefinitely against any siege.

With the march of time, the old fortress became the centrepiece in a succession of wars and invasions. There was the Albigensian War in 1208, the siege of Simon de Montfort, and the subsequent capture of the Castle by English invaders in the year 1360. In 1369 an attempt by the French under Du Guesclin to recapture the Castle met with failure, and it was not until the year 1377 that Gaston Phœbus was able to win it back for the King of France. Even so, the English were not completely driven out until the year 1407.

The Castle again figured prominently at the time of the Religious Wars. From 1569 to 1607, the Castle was taken and retaken by successive powers. As local Protestants from Béarn, led by Henry IV, warred with the Catholics of Bigorre in a conflict of mutual extermination, the poor town of Lourdes was captured and recaptured, sacked and pillaged.

The wars at last came to an end. In 1789 the Castle became a state prison, and continued to be used as such during the French Revolution until it was finally converted into an army barracks.

Today, now fully restored, it is a beautiful museum of the Pyrenees and holds annual exhibitions which revive the life and folklore of this marvellous land. Its old chapel contains original and opulent statues from the ancient church of Lourdes, unfortunately demolished at the beginning of the century.

One can see what is left of ancient Lourdes from its surrounding walls. A tangle of narrow streets and poor little houses cluster tightly together. In one of these narrow streets known as the « Petits Fossés » stands the little hovel, the now famous « Cachot » where Bernadette lived, and which over 400,000 pilgrims come annually to visit and to contemplate with great emotion.

With the emergence of France as a unified nation, ruled by the iron will of the Emperor Napoleon the First, the country was divided up and organized into departments. In this new France the day of the warlord and adventurer was at an end. A new aristocracy emerged and was composed of civil servants, tradesmen and state officials.

Lourdes, now a small provincial town, had nothing in its present make up to boast about and was left to dream of its past. In the structural reorganisation of the country the village had been bypassed in favour of the neighbouring town of Argelès. It was Argelès, situated a few miles away, and set in a pleasant and sunny valley, that was favoured to grow in stature and importance. Moreover, caught in a crossfire of hot and cold winds blowing from south to north down the Lavedan valley, and from east to west up from the River Gave, Lourdes, at an altitude of 430 m, could not be considered as an ideal place for holidays.

From spring to fall the inhabitants of Lourdes watched sadly as large stage coaches passed them on their way to Cauterets, Barèges and Luz-St-Sauveur, carrying the wealthy aristocracy and bourgeoisie to « take of the thermal waters » and to make rich the owners of the many hotels these towns could boast of. Hotels such as the « Hotel des Princes », the « Hotel Imperial » and the « Hotel de Londres » hosted a number of lords and landed gentry, artists and women of the world who lived in great style, a fact which left the Mayor of Lourdes and its populace looking on with envy.

Lourdes, however, had its own « High Society ». The town had its law courts. Magistrates and lawyers, public prosecutor and commissioner, all upheld respect for the law. Army officers commanded a detachment of soldiers both at Vizens and in the Castle, while a number of civil servants ensured imperial administration duties.

Its weekly market attracted the surrounding populace. The « Société » of leading villagers met each other at the Café Français as « enlightened men », unlike the little people of the « lower class ». The poor had their own drinking places and inns. Here quarrymen, stone carvers, millers, peasants and simple workers, who hired out their labour for a mere pittance, could come together and meet. One or two beggars were even included in the town register. Not everyone voted. Only a certain income could make this possible. Amongst the poor there was the poorest family of all : the Soubirous.

Cauterets : Gaube lake

Donkey riding (Cirque de Gavarnie) ▶

1

2

3

4

5

6

« They are poor, as poor as our Lord »

This was how Antoinette Tardhivail, a saintly girl living near the « Cachot », described, in late March 1858, the misfortune of the Soubirous. Their misfortune was real ; the family suffered severe hardship. But their misery, in the light of events to come, was not that of a people down on their luck, of people who « didn't know how to manage » or who were « good for nothings ». Theirs was a more priviledged kind of poverty, a poverty which in the light of their life story and in the light of God's providence, mirrored the very message of the Gospels. The Good News is about God coming towards us not in power but as a beggar of love ; a God heralded in Nazareth and born in a stable in Bethlehem « since there was no room for them at the inn ».

Nazareth - The Grotto of the Holy Family

Bethlehem - The shepherd's cave

Poverty, far from being a curse, is, with the coming of Jesus Christ, a Sign of God ; it calls the rich to their senses and reminds the poor of their dignity.

EVANGELICAL POVERTY IS THE FIRST POINT OF THE MESSAGE OF LOURDES.

At the age of 36 years François Soubirous, a miller by trade, married the much younger blue-eyed blonde Louise Castérot who was only 18 at the time. The marriage was celebrated on January 9th 1843, and led to a period spanning ten years during which the couple enjoyed a simple happiness. Even the usual domestic wrangles with in-laws that is common to most marriages, and which was present in theirs, did not affect the deep love between François and Louise.

One year later, on **January 9th 1844, 2 days after her birth**, Bernadette was baptized. And life flowed on smoothly like the waters of the Lapaca river which turned the millstones of the Boly mill. It was the mill of happiness for a household who lived with a simple faith rooted in solid Christian traditions.

An accident in November 1844 momentarily interrupted this happiness. Madame Soubirous received a burn to her breast and Bernadette had to be entrusted to a wet-nurse at Bartrès for a period of 18 months.

In 1854 Bernadette was 10 years old. After a mainly happy childhood, that stood her in good stead for the rest of her life, a shower of misfortune now fell upon her. Firstly her father lost an eye in an accident while repairing his millstone. Then, round about the feast of St. John, the family, unable to pay their rent, was forced to leave the mill where they had enjoyed so much happiness. The generosity and kind-heartedness of the miller in giving credit to the poor had led to their downfall. They fared no better at the Baudéan mill.

1

2 LE CACHOT

15

3

In the autumn of 1855 cholera swept through the town and caused 38 deaths within the space of a few weeks. Bernadette was stricken by the disease and almost died. The effects of this plague were to leave her with asthma for the rest of her life. And once more the family was forced to change mill and move to Arcizac. But there bad crops followed them, and without crops, without wheat, there was no work for a miller. The family was bankrupt !

1856 : Lourdes was the victim of famine.

The Emperor, on holiday in Biarritz, was caught up in the affair and sent the army with carts of flour to be distributed to the poor. Soubirous, the master miller, now became a « brassier » or day labourer. When work was to be found, he hired out his strength for the meagre sum of 1,20 francs a day (the daily hire of a horse was 1,50 francs !). Louise, Bernadette's mother, washed clothes or worked as a farmhand in order to earn them some money.

Bernadette stayed at home to look after her little brothers and sisters. No more school. No more catechism class. The first duty was to survive !

1857 : So that there was one less mouth to feed, Bernadette took up work as a maid in an inn. But not even this improved their situation. Without the means to pay the meagre rent for the little hovel in which they lived they were forced to leave the premises. Their future home was now to become the « Cachot », an old gaol abandoned for sanitary reasons in 1824, a place truly unfit for human habitation. Their cousin Sajous let them live there free of rent in this hovel which he owned in the « Rue des Petits Fossés ».

On **March 27th 1857** calamity struck again. François Soubirous was arrested by the gendarmes. Two sacks of flour had been stolen from Maisongrosse the baker : « it was his destitution that made me think it could have been him » admitted the plaintif. It was later proved that he was not guilty, but Soubirous

Saint Michael Garicoïts

Father Michael Garicoïts, an extraordinary character whose holiness was renowned throughout the region, sometimes visited the Boly Mill.

There he was given sacks of flour for the poor for whom he worked unceasingly.

In the difficulties that often weighed heavily upon the newly married Soubirous, he was an instrument of peace and enlightenment.

The « Saint of Betharram » as he was called, appears again in the life of the Soubirous after the Apparitions.

For both the Bishop, who held him in great esteem, and for Bernadette who was sent to him, Michael Garicoïts was a wise, discerning and discreet counsellor.

Saint Michael Garicoïts

The Shrine of Betharram

nevertheless had to spend eight days in prison.

In the face of such trials one can only imagine the despair that must have hung over the Cachot, and the anguish which this 13 year old girl Bernadette must have experienced in her heart. The coming winter augured further hardships. Once again, to have « one less mouth to feed », Bernadette was sent as a farmhand to work at her nurse's farm at Bartrès. Instead of the school and catechism promised her for the preparation of her first Communion, she herded pigs and sheep and did domestic chores.

Bernadette was solidly with her family in whatever troubles came their way. She did not add her sadness to theirs. In the simple faith she possessed she found the strength which kept her from falling into the ways of a stubborn, dreamy, or rebellious adolescent. With astonishing clarity she said : « When you know that something is allowed to happen by God, you don't complain about it. »

There was something, though, that she couldn't accept. And this was being kept away from what she needed for her faith as a Christian : the right to learn to read, so that she could study her catechism, a necessary task before receiving first Holy Communion. The gentle Bernadette now revealed her character and her decisiveness. She succeeded in getting her family's permission to return to Lourdes, and skilfully managed to convince Madame Laguès, her mistress, to let her leave Bartrès. « The Parish Priest of Lourdes wants me to make my first Communion » she told her.

January 20th 1858 : she returned to live in the misery and squalor of the Cachot, and attended a convent-run school where she was put in a « pauper's class » with no fees to pay, in the company of children from 7 to 8 years of age. Courageous Bernadette !

« What is poor, what is little, this is what God has chosen... » Three weeks later **February 11th 1858** dawned.

Inside the « cachot »

Inside the house at Bartrès ▶

From the darkness came the Light

A dark and sombre sky hung over the icy cold morning of **Thursday 11th February**. Outside the Cachot there was mist and drizzling rain. Inside, the family shivered from the cold and damp. The last of the firewood had gone, the last bundle having been sold the night before to buy food. Bernadette pleaded with her mother to be allowed to go and fetch some. Afraid that the bad weather might cause Bernadette an attack of asthma, her mother was at first reluctant, but finally gave way to her daughter's constant pleading.

And so it was that Bernadette, her sister Toinette and a friend Jeanne Abadie, nicknamed Baloum, made their way to the river Gave. They crossed the meadow of the Savy mill (the present day Rosary Square). « We are not thieves » said Bernadette as they crossed this private property and left untouched the many fallen branches that lay strewn there. Further on they came to the « pig-sty », a rocky recess where the river currents washed up driftwood and all sorts of rubbish. This place had often been a treasure trove for these poor children who sold what they found to the local rag market in Lourdes. Even that very day they were to find and to sell enough to buy 20 sous worth of bread, and this in a place used by Samson, the local swineherd, as a watering hole for pigs.

Heaven certainly has its ways ! What a sign for those who can read beyond appearances. But let us listen to how Bernadette herself described the events which left such an indelible impression on her heart, and which she wrote about several times over in almost identical terms. Here is the first account, written on May 28th 1861, at a time when Bernadette was just learning to write :

The grotto in 1858 (as it was at the time of the Apparitions)

« I was on my way to gather wood on the banks of the Gave with two other girls. They crossed the stream and began to cry. I asked them why they were crying and they answered that the water was icy cold. I begged them to help me throw stones into the water so I could cross without having to take off my shœs but they answered that I would have to do as they had done. So I went a little further on to see if there was a place to cross with my shœs on. But there was nowhere to cross. I then came back in front of the Grotto to take my shœs off. Just as I was beginning to do so I heard a noise. I turned towards the meadow and I saw that the trees stood perfectly still. I carried on taking off my shœs and all of a sudden I heard the same noise again. I looked up towards the Grotto and I saw a Lady dressed in white : she had on a white dress with a blue belt and a yellow rose on each foot, the colour of her rosary. When I saw this I rubbed my eyes for I thought I was mistaken. I put my hand in my pocket and found my rosary beads. I wanted to make the sign of the cross but couldn't raise my hand to my forehead. The vision crossed herself. My hand trembled, then I tried to do it too and I succeeded. I took out my rosary ; the vision let the beads of her own run through her fingers, but still her lips did not move. When I had finished saying the rosary, the vision suddenly vanished. I asked the other two little girls if they had seen anything but they replied that they had not. They asked me what had happened and that I had to tell them. So I told them that I had seen a Lady dressed in white, but that I didn't know who it was and I asked them to tell no one about this. »

Toinette and Baloum promised not to say anything about it, but within the space of a few hours the story had become common knowledge throughout the entire town. Madame Soubirous, overcome with worry and fear, was angry and punished Bernadette, forbidding her to return to the Grotto. At school, tongues wagged. In Lourdes, gossip spread. As it was carnival time in the village, many wrote it off as a « prank ».

Sunday 14th February dawned and Bernadette, the gentle and powerful call from the cave at Massabielle locked deep in her heart, was taken there by her school friends who somehow managed to get permission from the Soubirous to do so. With a phial of holy water for protection the children hurried off towards the « pig-sty ». Bernadette met the Lady for a second time. Upon seeing her, Bernadette fell into a rapture of fantastic joy which astonished the children and made several adults come running, such as Nicolau the miller who worked nearby. Louise Soubirous was sent for and arrived, stick in hand, and firmly and decisively forbade her daughter ever to return to this unhappy cave : « It's all just an illusion, I never want her to return here », she cried.

On Thursday 18th February Bernadette was again found at the Grotto, before dawn, with Madame Milhet a rich lady who sometimes provided work for Louise and some bread for the family. She had gained permission to secretly accompany Bernadette to the meeting place at Massabielle. Miss Peyret, the daughter of the public notary, was also present with pen and paper so that Bernadette could ask the Lady to sign her name.

Facsimile of the account of the first Apparition

The Lady smiled at this quaint demand from the illiterate Bernadette and said :

« WHAT I HAVE TO SAY TO YOU NEED NOT BE TAKEN DOWN IN WRITING. »

In a more serious tone, she spoke her first important message :

« WOULD YOU BE KIND ENOUGH TO COME HERE FOR FIFTEEN DAYS.

« I CANNOT PROMISE TO MAKE YOU HAPPY IN THIS WORLD BUT IN THE OTHER. »

An unknown happiness, the happiness of the « other world » invaded Bernadette's heart and she promised to come faithfully. Bernadette's joy was contagious and spread to the others present at the Apparitions, who, although they saw nothing, could not help but have the feeling of a presence. Bernadette was later to say : « She looked at me as one person looks at another ; she spoke to me in my own native tongue ».

The dark gloomy « pig-sty », part of the mountain of Massabielle, became a place of light and joy, revealing « the other world », just like Mt. Tabor where Jesus « Son of the carpenter » transfigured in light revealed himself as Son of God.

Mt. Tabor

« How glad was my soul, good Mother... when I gazed upon you »

These words were found in a notebook written by Bernadette eight years later. The happiness promised to Bernadette by Our Lady was not only intended for life after death ; it is a happiness experienced by all those who progress in the way of prayer - who go beyond the utterance of prayerful words to the discovery of true Prayer. It was this experience that Bernadette came to discover as she knelt before Our Lady. She went beyond the mere recitation of the rosary to savour the deeper experience of a warm and loving communion, « of a friend speaking to a friend ». There before the Grotto, Bernadette's deeply prayerful experience silently touched the hearts of all who watched, and crowds began to form in ever greater numbers as the famous FORTNIGHT OF APPARITIONS progressed.

On **Friday 19th February** eight people were present, including Madame Soubirous and Bernadette's aunt Bernarde who also happened to be her godmother. In spite of their natural fear, they found comfort in the calm happiness displayed by Bernadette throughout this fourth Apparition. Bernadette was armed with a candle as a final protection.

On Saturday 20th February, thirty people were in attendance and returned to the village deeply moved and astonished at the extraordinary atmosphere of peace and joy that emanated from the poor little Grotto.

Father Pène, the local parish curate, questioned Bernadette about the happiness she found at the Grotto. She answered : « When I see her I feel as if I'm no longer of this world. And when the vision disappears I'm amazed to find myself still here. »

On **Sunday 21st** numbers had risen to well over one hundred. The police began to keep an eye on the place ; they counted the crowd and were truly alarmed by events. Jacomet, the Police Commissioner, sent for Bernadette, questioned her, threatened her, and finally obtained from François Soubirous, who had no desire to return to prison, the assurance that the whole business would cease. Bernadette's sadness upset her familly (« she is no liar », said her mother).

Monday 22nd arrived and Bernadette, in obedience to the will of her father, painfully went off to school. But then in the afternoon of that same day an irresistable force drew her back to Massabielle. There was however no Apparition.

On **Tuesday 23rd**, in spite of the Police Commissioner, Bernadette was back again at the Grotto for the seventh Apparition. There was but a small gathering of people that included some of the leading villagers who had come out of curiosity and the desire to mock the gullibility of the « lower classes ».

A certain Jean-Baptiste Estrade, a tax inspector with a rather aloof personality, was also present, sent by the Parish Priest Father Peyramale to « find out what was going on ». He and Duffo, the court official, with officers from the garrison and other eminent citizens, had come to witness this « Mardi Gras carnival on the advice of the Parish Priest ». But instead of being shocked or scandalised, they were astonished and moved by the whole experience. The vision of Bernadette in prayer turned them into « believers and witnesses ».

Something was definitely happening at Massabielle.

There was no stopping it now. The « pigsty » was about to become the « Blessed Grotto » a place destined to make of Lourdes the « Capital of Prayer » in which the Message of Prayer would take root and flourish.

« How good it is to be here »

The Café Français, the meeting place of the local intelligentsia, was alive with gossip and rumour following the happenings at the Grotto as related by Estrade and his colleagues. The bourgeoisie constantly indulged in discussing the pros and cons of the affair. In any event, whether from curiosity or scepticism, people continued to flock to the Grotto. Estrade, a regular theatre goer, commented that « Bernadette in ecstasy was more beautiful than Rachel, the famous actress, ever was even at the height of her career ».

The Commissioner's office and the police authorities prudently left matters alone. Their only action was to list the numbers and names of those present and to send off reports of the events to higher authorities.

The Soubirous family were for the moment surprisingly treated with some degree of consideration. Aunt Bernarde stood firmly by the visionary, her goddaughter, the « little Saint » as she began to be called at Lourdes. But it was then that drama occurred once more.

Bernadette and the Castle

« She seemed to carry all the sorrow of the world upon her shoulders... »

These words spoken by Marie Pailhes, a simple woman who closely observed Bernadette throughout this period, seem to express the essence of what now took place.

Wednesday 24th February : 250 people clustered around Bernadette taking up all the space between the River Gave and the rock of Massabielle. Sadness and tears stained the transfigured face of the visionary. The message given today was repeated at the Grotto and in the town :

« PENANCE ! »

« PRAY FOR THE CONVERSION OF SINNERS. »

And how good it was to pray at Massabielle. People arrived earlier than ever. In the cold of winter, they were happy to be there, by the banks of the River Gave, to « watch and pray ».

Thursday 25th February : the police recorded a crowd of more than 350. Hoping to witness something of her ecstasy, the huge crowd waited with eagerness for Bernadette's arrival. Unlike the fine weather of previous days, this was a cold miserable rainy day. It was out of the cold misty dawn that Bernadette finally appeared. She was seen to remove her hood, put her candle aside, walk towards the Gave, then turn, go down on her kness and finally crawl on all fours to the back of the Grotto, towards the left of the rock.

When she rose and turned towards the crowd what a surprise they got. There she was, her face unrecognisable, smeared with mud, and chewing a tuft of grass gathered up from the muddy ground of the Grotto.

« What in heaven's name is Bernadette up to ? »

« Has she gone mad ? »

The surprise and consternation of the onlookers soon turned to resentment, sarcasm and anger. People were shocked and horrified. Banner headlines in the next day's papers angrily proclaimed that « the gullible have been well and truly had », and added vehemently that « Bernadette's real place should be in the asylum ». At the Grotto itself on the day of the incident, it was Aunt Bernarde, acting as head of the family who intervened. « Stop your nonsense » she cried, as she soundly slapped Bernadette's face and sent her off towards the Cachot to the mocking jeers of those present.

« An unforgettably gloomy day » wrote Estrade, who now had to suffer the taunts and jibes of his colleagues of the Café Français. Furious at having let themselves be dragged into this misadventure, they were equally enraged to discover that one supposedly more beautiful than Rachel was no more than a « filthy little upstart ».

« Filthy », the term was repeatedly used throughout the town to conjure up the image of Bernadette covered with the mud and dung of the « pig-sty ». As was to be expected, the local authorities grasped the changed mood and atmosphere of the village and reacted quickly. That very same evening, Bernadette was summoned to appear before Dutour, the Imperial Public Prosecutor, by no means a pleasant prospect since this was the « nice » gentleman who had put Bernadette's father in prison !

For two long hours, on her feet all the time and with her mother also standing beside her, the young girl endured a grilling interrogation. She was questioned and further questioned, accused and threatened, attacked and bombarded with all kinds of insinuations... until her mother, weakened by fear and sorrow, fainted. The accused were at last shown two chairs to sit in.

While her mother flopped into one chair, Bernadette refused the other. « No I would soil it », she said, and chose rather to sit on the floor, displaying as she did so, all the pride of a mountain girl in defiance of the condescending air of the Prosecutor.

After a few final words of intimidation and threat of imprisonment, the two women were released. Bernadette consoled her mother as she said : « You see, we have done nothing wrong at all ».

In the midst of this general turmoil Bernadette remained calm and displayed a kind of serious-ness that was quite new to her. She explained her odd behaviour at the Grotto to whœver wanted to listen to her. She had cried the day before « because the Lady was sad » while speaking of sinners. This morning the Lady had also said :

« WOULD YOU KISS THE GROUND AND CRAWL ON YOUR KNEES FOR SINNERS ? »

« WOULD YOU EAT THE GRASS THAT IS THERE FOR SINNERS ? »

The Agony - a Mosaic of the Rosary Basilica

« GO AND DRINK FROM THE SPRING AND WASH YOURSELF THERE. »

Let us listen to Bernadette's own account of events :

« I first made for the Gave but she told me that this was not the place, and then she pointed out with her finger where I ought to go. I went but found only a little pool of dirty water. I dipped my hand in but could not cup any so I started to scrape the earth away and I was able to take some. Three times I threw it away ; the fourth time I managed to drink some. She added that I must pray for sinners. »

For Bernadette, all this had meaning and purpose. Only a few rare people, such as Marie Pailhes, moved by the sadness written upon Bernadette's face, had grasped the full gravity of the situation. « She seemed to carry all the sorrow of the world », wrote Marie Pailhes.

But as for the majority, they had unfeelingly behaved like the many Jews who, on Good Friday, had abandoned a certain Jesus of Nazareth, whom, only a few days before, they had so admired and loved. On that Good Friday,

---

The 9th Apparition is really the culminating point of the Lourdes message

The water oozing from the inner recesses of the Grotto was now to take on an unimaginably deep meaning. So much more than a mere purifying water which may sometimes produce miraculous cures. This water is the mystical Sign of the water that flowed with the Blood from Christ's side, gashed by the soldier's spear. An enlightening coincidence ; it was remembered that in the catholic Liturgy being said at the time of the events there was an episode of the Passion (see the Altar book used at the time in the Lourdes parish).

Yes, without knowing it and as yet without understanding, Bernadette had mimed the Passion « for sinners ».

He who had drawn such crowds was now disfigured, stricken, scourged and crowned with thorns. Among all those who « turned away from him shaking their heads », who was to remember the Biblical prophecy of a Suffering Servant of God, « one with no look to attract our eyes », who would become « a worm and no man » as the psalmist puts it. Even the friends of Jesus failed to understand that « ours were the sufferings he carried, and ours the sorrows he bore ». Yet they had lived with Him and He had tried to teach them this.

Only the evening before, in the midst of lengthy explanations, Jesus had taken a loaf of bread and said : « this is my body given up for sinners. » He had taken a cup of wine and said : « this is my blood poured out for all men. » Jesus had not wanted this cross, this passion ; three times he had said to his Father « let this cup pass from me ». But He finally surrendered himself to his Father : « May your will be done. »

Who could have fathomed the depths of this passionate love Jesus had for sinners, and towards what cruel suffering it was to lead Him, the innocent Lamb, who took upon himself all the sins of the world.

For centuries the paschal lamb of the Jews had been offered to God at each Passover feast in memory of their liberation from Egypt. Now in his passion, Jesus revealed himself as the true Lamb of God come to bring about a more radical liberation - the liberation of all mankind from sin. What insight upon this grass that Bernadette found « difficult and bitter » to eat.

On this day of the 9th Apparition, it was Christ's passion for sinners that Bernadette, in contemplating the sadness and message of Mary, came to discover. During the course of her life, she would meditate upon and deepen her understanding of this mystery ; her compassion and prayer for « poor sinners », and her humble solidarity with them, was to grow ever more profound until the very moment of

her death when her last words were « Pray for me, for I am a poor sinner ».

For the time being, Bernadette came to realise that beyond her immediate concerns, beyond her personal and family problems, there existed a worse poverty and misery than that of the Cachot, and a greater violence than the opposition she was then experiencing. The terrible world of sin dramatically invaded her heart and consciousness. It was this mud of the world, this ugliness of evil, which, as she often said throughout her life, horribly disfigured the faces of all « poor sinners, our brothers ».

The message of Penance that Bernadette now began to convey to others went far beyond the practice of a few humiliating and ascetic gestures such as can be found in all religions. The Penance that the Lady of Massabielle had spoken of was that true conversion of heart, which, in contemplating Jesus upon the Cross, understands the true nature of sin, and finds in the passion of God's love for the lost, the way to personal and collective salvation.

On the next day, Friday 26th February, having returned once more to the Grotto, Bernadette experienced a heaviness and emptiness of heart, much as that experienced by the disciples on Holy Saturday when all seemed to have come to an end.

But far from coming to an end, everything was just about to begin. Water began to flow from the spring Bernadette had discovered, and with the occurrence of a few spectacular miracles the fortnight of Apparitions resumed with a new fervour and air of expectancy that grew stronger each day.

On Saturday 27th February 800 people were present for the 10th Apparition.

And on Sunday 28th the crowd was bigger still with some 1150 people there. The authorities were concerned.

Renault, Commanding Officer of the police squadron, came from Tarbes to see for himself what measures were needed to control such a huge crowd massed dangerously by the river's edge.

Judge Ribes brought Bernadette in for further questioning and tried once more to discourage her from going to the Grotto. But to no avail. Bernadette « had promised to go there for fifteen days ».

On **Monday 1st March**, a similar crowd gathered again in a spirit of peace, recollection and prayer. A priest, a Father Desirat, unaware of the laws issued by Fr. Peyramale outlawing attendance at the Grotto, was present next to Bernadette. He noted his impression of events : « What struck me was the joy, the sadness reflected in Bernadette's face... Respect, silence, recollection reigned everywhere. Oh it was so good to be there ! It was like being at the gates of Paradise. »

Indeed that very same day, at dawn, a little of Paradise had come into the life of someone present at the Grotto. Catherine Latapie, pregnant for 9 months, had walked the 9 km from her village of Loubajac to bathe her paralysed arm in the waters at the Grotto.

Not only did she leave the Grotto healed, but having just arrived back home, she gave birth to her third child : Jean-Baptiste.

Her healing was the first miracle of Lourdes to be recognised and was considered as a sign of the truth of the Apparitions. (Episcopal Commission of 1862).

Back at the Parish, the clergy remained suspicious and reticent about the whole affair although they acknowledged the astounding number of conversions that were taking place. What was to be thought of it all ?

« Go and tell... »

March 2nd, the day of the 15th Apparition dawned. At the end of her ecstasy Bernadette heard the Lady say :

« GO AND TELL THE PRIEST TO BUILD A CHAPEL HERE AND TO HAVE PEOPLE COME IN PROCESSION. »

A divine request no doubt, and yet the task that lay before Bernadette was both formidable and intimidating. A visit to the Parish Priest had always been a daunting task at the best of times. Father Peyramale was not known as an easy-going character. His awesome personality was matched by an equally awesome voice, and it was common knowledge that he had grown impatient and weary of this Grotto story.

Yet, full of love and courage, Bernadette resolved to do as the Lady had requested. With her two aunts Bernarde and Basile, whom she somehow convinced to join her, in spite of their own natural fears of the Parish Priest, Bernadette set off on her way to brave ecclesiastical authority. The support of meek old Father Pomian, the curate, had been hoped for, but without success. And so here they were at last, these three women, three laywomen, simple « children of Mary[1] » in front of the presbytery.

They were given an icy reception. Bernadette hardly had the time to utter half her message when the storm broke upon her. « Little liar », cried the priest, « what a misfortune it is to have a family creating havoc in the parish ». Furious and enraged, he cast a chilling glance at the two aunts. « Lock her up »,

he commanded, « stop her from going back to this cave ». Stunned, the two aunts headed for the door. Bernadette followed, deeply troubled. The Parish priest's anger had prevented Bernadette from giving all of her message. She was unable to speak of the « Chapel ».

Shrugging off this obstacle, Bernadette, with courage and determination, managed, in the end, to deliver her message. She went off to find Dominiquette Cazenave who had a way with the stolid priest, and that very evening she was received at the presbytery and questioned in the presence of the entire parish clergy. Bernadette withheld nothing and had an answer for every question. That night she left the rectory bouncing with joy, and said : « I am so happy, my errand is done. .

Without realising it Bernadette had just lived through an important and decisive day so reminiscent of the day of the Resurrection itself. That day too had started badly with shattered hopes and discouraged hearts. And then when all seemed lost, all began.

On that day, another woman, Mary Magdalene, had gone to the tomb, a tomb which seemed to suggest the definite end of the prophet Jesus. But then the tomb was discovered empty - and suddenly an order was given to her : « Go and tell Peter and the other Apostles... » She, the sinner, was to give the Good News to these men crushed by despair. For Bernadette, as for Mary Magdalene, the message was the same : a Church, the People of God was to be built around the presence of the Risen and living Christ.

---

1 : Bernadette's two aunts had almost been excluded from the « children of Mary » because of public scandal, a pregnancy outside marriage.

Who was Fr. Peyramale ?

He who came to be known as the « priest of the Apparitions » was from a background much different to that of Bernadette.

He was born in a well-off household that can still be seen today in the main square of the village of Momères. Marie-Dominique Peyramale came from a highly respected and cultured family which had long associations in the field of medicine and law.

One of his brothers was a doctor, another was a government official. A third brother became Director of the Ministry of Finance in Peru having gone into exile there after the Revolution of 1830. His daughter, Delphine Peyramale, became part of the family of Garcia Moreno, the famous president of the Republic of Mexico.

Fr. Peyramale, having completed a successful ministry as curate, parish priest, and then chaplain to the garrison and military hospital at Tarbes, became Parish priest in Lourdes in 1855.

His education, his connections, his dynamic character and his great charity quickly established him as a person of great authority. When poor Bernadette went from the Cachot, the miserable hovel where she and her family had taken refuge, to fearfully deliver to him « Our Lady's message », the contrast between them must have been startling...

God certainly has his ways.

Fr. Peyramale

Peyramale's family home at Momères

« Ask her to tell us her name »

Following his encounter with Bernadette, Father Peyramale felt more puzzled than ever, not only on account of his own questioning, but also because his own curates could no longer agree among themselves. Some like Father Pène, favouring Bernadette's story, were keen and enthusiastic, and failed to understand the reticence of their Parish Priest. Others like Bernadette's confessor, the prudent and reserved Father Pomian, preferred to wait for further developments.

Peyramale decided it was time to pay a visit to Tarbes to see the Bishop, His Excellency Mgr Laurence. From his own hand we have an account of the conversation :

« I said to His Excellency : « some say that we too should go to the Grotto. »

Bishop Laurence

« Well, what are you waiting for ? » said His Excellency.

« But some say that if we do go, we'll be accused of stirring things up »

« Oh, really ? Well, don't go then. » concluded the Bishop.

With Peyramale locked in such deep perplexity it came as no surprise to find Bernadette, returning after the 14th Apparition to repeat her message, being given a cool reception.

« If the Lady wants her chapel, let her tell you her name, and ask her to make the rosebush at the Grotto flower », said Peyramale more irritated than usual on that evening of March 3rd on account of the growing unrest taking place around him. Excitement in the town had reached fever pitch. All day long thousands of curious people had come flocking into Lourdes eager for the arrival of Thursday, the last day of the fortnight of Apparitions, and for the signs and wonders this day might bring.

The Prefect and Imperial Prosecutor, the Mayor and Police Commissioner, officers and soldiers, and the police forces of Lourdes and the neighbouring towns of St-Pé and Argelès had all been alerted. The priest had been informed and had given approval. The Grotto was searched inside out and a guard was posted there throughout the night.

Bernadette spent a peaceful night at the « Cachot ». At daybreak, three doctors from Bordeaux came to examine her. If she could be found to be mad and interned somewhere, all this turmoil would be ended and peace would return. They tried in vain. The doctors found nothing abnormal in the child. In fact, on seeing the filthy hovel where the family lived, they were obliged to declare to Madame Soubirous : « If you want to keep your children alive, then don't stay here too long. » Later on March 27th, by order of the Prefect and the Mayor, Bernadette was examined again, this time by three Lourdes doctors who came to the same conclusion as those before them : Bernadette's mental health was unquestionably sound.

On the morning of **March 4th**, having attended Mass for a dead relative, Bernadette set out for what might be her last meeting with the Lady. Serene and recollected, she made her way through an immense crowd later estimated to have been around 10,000 strong. Bernadette went into a rapturous ecstasy that lasted well over an hour in an atmosphere of fervour and peace that rendered unnecessary the attendant forces of law and order.

Those who had come along hoping to witness some passionate display of unbridled emotion were disappointed. Bernadette returned, quietly and deep in thought to the Cachot followed by the crowd who wanted to see and touch the « Saint ». Rumours of healings and miracles were rife. Bernadette was tired. She refused the enthusiastic adulation of the crowds, opposed the starring role she was expected to play, and vehemently refused

Fr Peyramale and Bernadette - Stained glass window

the gifts of money people tried to slip into her hand : « It burns me ! » she said.

Her only desire was to see the priest again, and somehow managing to slip away from the crowds she reached the presbytery :

« What did the Lady say to you then ? » asked Peyramale.

« I asked her name... and she smiled. I asked her to make the rosebush flower and she smiled again. But she still wants the chapel », answered Bernadette.

« And you, do you have the money to build this chapel ? »

« No Reverend Father, I do not. »

« Neither do I... Tell the Lady to give it to you. »

Was the story of Lourdes to end here, on this day of shattered hopes in which nothing spectacular seemed to have taken place ? With the evening fast approaching the crowds gradually dwindled away and without incident. As the forces of law and order relaxed, the priest remained troubled.

On March 18th Bernadette submitted to another formal interrogation and was questioned by the authorities about the so called miracles and about her intentions : « I do not believe », she declared, « that I have cured anyone and, for that matter, I have done nothing to that end. I do not know if I'll ever go back to the Grotto again ».

Three weeks went by. Although crowds still flocked fervently to the Grotto, the period marked Bernadette's return to a peaceful normality. Quietly she took up the humdrum routine of her daily life, going back to school where she endeavoured to « fill her poor little head » with the letters of the alphabet and the difficult formulas of the catechism.

Thursday 25th March : The NAME...

In the small hours of **March 25th**, at four o'clock in the morning, Bernadette was roused from her sleep by that now familiar irresistable urge to go to the Grotto. The coming day was an important one in the life of the Church. It was the feast of the Annunciation, a feast recalling how the Angel Gabriel had appeared to a young girl from Nazareth in the humble dwelling where she lived with her poor family, and made to her the momentous announcement that she was to become the Mother of the Saviour. On that day the Angel had given Mary a new name : « Mary, full of grace. »

On this feast of the Annunciation, at the Grotto in joyful reunion with her « young Lady », Bernadette firmly resolved to obtain the name so often requested and longed for by the Parish Priest. With her characteristic stubborness she repeated four times, stammering and stuttering as she did so, the phrase she had for so long prepared : « Mademoiselle, would you please be kind enough to tell me who you are. »

At the fourth request, the Lady stopped smiling, slipped her rosary on to her right arm, and with her hands joined she raised her eyes to heaven and said :

« I AM THE IMMACULATE CONCEPTION. »

Bernadette's joy was immense. Full of gratitude, she felt moved to leave something in this wonderful place. So she took the candle she had been carrying and placed it between two rocks where it could remain as a symbol of her continued and ardent prayer. Bernadette now hurried off to the presbytery continually repeating these strange and wonderful words :

« I am the Immaculate Conception. »

Finally she arrived at the rectory and blurted out the name to Father Peyramale. « A woman cannot have a name like that », he answered, « you are mistaken. Do you know what that means ? »

Bernadette shook her head. She had no idea of the meaning of this strange title. She had never heard these words before and had been obliged to repeat them on her way from the Grotto to the presbytery lest she forgot them. Peyramale was clearly chocked with emotion almost to the point of tears « Go home », he said to the child, « I'll see you another day ». Bernadette left still ignorant as to the meaning of the Lady's words. It was only later on, in the afternoon, while she was at Estrade's house, that she was told how the Blessed Virgin carried such a title. Bernadette experienced great joy. « She could never have invented this », wrote Peyramale to his Bishop that same evening.

The message of Lourdes had been signed.

16th Apparition - Upper Basilica stained glass window

The Message of Lourdes

The message of Lourdes is not limited to the words Bernadette heard at the Grotto. It has been handed down to us, as we have just seen, within the fabric of a history woven around situations, characters, events and acts which have as much and at times even more impact than the actual words themselves.

The Apparitions at Massabielle both encompass and surpass the exchanges which took place between Mary and Bernadette. They point to a wider horizon. They direct us to that fundamental and indispensable context in the light of which every message from God has to be read : that of the Gospels. As we follow in Bernadette's footsteps this is where we are led - to the Gospel.

Firstly we discover **poverty**.

Poverty, for this is the sign of God's presence. He comes to us, not in a wondrous and mighty glory that would blind our eyes, but in a poverty that allows Him to draw close to our hearts. Before the Apparitions Bernadette accepted life with a certain kind of stoic resignation, albeit deeply motivated by faith : « You shouldn't complain », she would say. But after the Apparitions, when she realised more deeply the ways of God and read her life story in the light of His providence she went beyond this to say : « I want to remain poor » It was the answer she gave to anyone and everyone who wanted to take her out of this condition, like the journalist who wanted to take her to Paris where, in relating the story of the Apparitions, she could have made herself a fortune.

In spite of her ignorance of the catechism, the light of the Apparitions enabled Bernadette to read the sense and purpose of all the poverty which she and her family experienced. Did they not resemble the true God, who, through Jesus, came as a poor man among the poor ? This is the first message of Lourdes.

Then we discover **true Prayer**.

The friendly meeting with the « little Lady », as she so often called her, revealed to Bernadette, and today reveals to us, that a God of love and tenderness is the image of the true God, a God who searches to embrace and to converse with men within a heart-to-heart encounter. True prayer is our response to this God and expresses our desire for a dialogue of love in which we too can talk to God « heart-to-heart ».

« Virgin of Light, You are the smile of a God who loves us. » So begins an evening hymn to Mary frequently sung at Lourdes. True prayer is this - to go beyond the mere recitation of words and discover « the smile of a God who loves us », to find ourselves in loving company with a God of tenderness. This is the second message of Lourdes.

Then we realise the true meaning of **Penance**.

The world in which we live is a hard, violent and at times hideous world. The disgusting mud of the « pig-sty » symbolizes it rather well. Bernadette, with her face disfigured by the mud of the pig-sty, becomes a symbol of the deep love that led Jesus to his Passion « for sinners ». She invites us to become aware of the true nature of sin, to see clearly the ugliness of evil and to courageously seek a true conversion of heart that goes far beyond the practise of a few occasional penances. True penance avoids the hypocrisy of the righteous for it enables us to see ourselves as the sinners that we are, and helps us, as we recognise our mutual misery, to be more compassionate towards each other. This is the third message of Lourdes.

Finally the **True Church**.
A human Church

The Church of Christ is today a Church made up of weak, limited sinners, just as it was in its beginnings when weak men like Peter and Paul left everything to follow Jesus. Today, the Church of Christ experiences, as it did then, persecution and abandonment. Lourdes tells us that the story of the Church continues.

It was not to Michael Garicoïts, whose extraordinary holiness earned him the title of the « Saint of Betharram » (and who was canonised by the Church after his death in 1863), that Bernadette was sent. Our Lady chose instead to send her to the Parish Priest, neither the best nor the worst of men, because it was he who represented in Lourdes the legitimate authority of the Church.

Michael Garicoïts himself, already convinced of the truth of the Apparitions, remained absolutely silent on the matter in deference to this ecclesiasical authority exercised by the Parish Priest of Lourdes and by the Bishop of Tarbes. It was for them to decide on the conduct of the Church in the affairs taking place in Lourdes, and decide they did. It was an undertaking which took them and their colleagues almost four years of painstaking study, careful thought and ardent prayer to accomplish. A lesson indeed for those today who would rush, without thought nor reason, to declare as « Apparition » the slightest rumour of the extraordinary !

In the story of the Apparitions it was Bernadette, a simple laywoman, who was chosen as the messenger of heaven and sent to the Church authorities. In her story we are reminded that in the true Church of Christ each of us has a role to play, simply, bravely and lovingly. We are reminded that this is the Church of men wanted by Christ, in which nobody has the right to remain a simple spectator. This is the fourth message of Lourdes

A Universal Church « on the move »

The word procession, in Lourdes dialect, means a pilgrimage outside of one's parish into other parishes to meet with the People of God on their way through world history.

Pilgrimage reminds us all that « we have no permanent abode here », and that since Abraham, « the father of believers », we are all « pilgrims » on the move, on our way to the promised land. It is this promised land of joy and forgiveness, of reconciliation and celebration that is symbolized by the crowds who gather in Lourdes at the foot of the chapel rising from the Rock of Massabielle.

Here, the nations of the Earth, continents and countries, young and old, the healthy and the sick meet in peace and brotherly love.

Here, all languages are spoken, all kinds of music are played. It could be the tower of Babel, in reality, it is more the event of Pentecost described in the Acts of the Apostles : « all persevered in prayer with Mary, the Mother of Jesus », and seized with the breath of the Spirit of God, « each adored God in his own tongue. »

A Church with Mary as Mother

Why was it Mary, the Woman, who came to Lourdes to remind us of the Gospel ? Was it not because a new humanity began with the Woman « blessed among all others ». the Virgin Mary, the « Immaculate Conception » : a new humanity in contrast to the old, that of Eve, the first woman, who brought evil into the world ?

With the Gospel everything begins anew. It heralds the beginning of the Church. It should come as no surprise to find the Mother there, looking after her children. Her name, the « IMMACULATE CONCEPTION », given at the Grotto, sums up the entire message of Lourdes.

③

But what became of Bernadette ?

Following the revelation of the Blessed Virgin's identity, Bernadette withdrew into the shadows of a simple routine life. She celebrated the feast of Easter, on April 4th, quietly but with great joy as she pondered the Lady's name and beheld in her heart the beautiful face that matched such a wondrous title. Just as everything seemed to have fallen into place, all of a sudden, on Easter Wednesday 7th April , Bernadette again felt drawn to the Grotto. She arrived early carrying a large candle. As usual, a few hundred people had already gathered to pray.

The unexpected arrival of Bernadette and the ecstasy that envelopped her, hushed the crowd to a prayerful stillness. But this atmosphere of prayer and recollection was not to last for long. A man noisily forced his way through the crowds to be at Bernadette's side. It was Dr. Douzous, a colourful character, whose early scepticism about the whole affair had given way to keen academic interest. Wishing to observe the phenomenon of Bernadette in ecstasy, he arrived on the scene, as he himself put it, « in the name of science ». At that moment, little did he realise

The candle as a symbol of Easter

On the day that the churches burn the Easter candle, a symbol of Christ announcing the resurrection, Bernadette made her own quiet sign of Easter at the 16th Apparition. It is perhaps of interest to remark that she was to die 21 years later, on Easter Wednesday.

Her body has remained intact, incorruptible, and may be seen at Nevers ; a last hint, a last sign of the Gospel here to bring men Resurrection and Life.

Candles at night

the role he was about to play as a primary witness of the « candle miracle ». The large candle that Bernadette held began to burn lower and lower until she was left holding nothing more than the wick. As the flames licked her fingers, Bernadette never budged. This lasted fully ten minutes, observed the doctor, astounded. When the ecstasy was over he examined Bernadette's hands. There were no traces of burning, even though the child was extremely sensitive to heat. Douzous went back to the police station where Commissioner Jacomet recorded his account in writing (see below) : « Now I believe the story », declared the doctor to all and sundry.

Bernadette experienced all this in a deep and hidden way. Like Mary « she pondered all these things in her heart » Even in the face of mounting excitement caused by the emergence of false visionaries, Bernadette remained calm and silent. In any case there was much for her to do. As poverty still plagued the Cachot, she helped with the housework and took up employment, in between her hours of school and catechism, as a « children's nanny ». In addition she was never free of the task of having to relate the story of the famous Fortnight, but did so in simplicity and in the briefest time possible !

In May, extremely tired and suffering from chronic asthma, she was taken three times to Cauterets. At last the long-awaited day of her first Communion arrived, Thursday 3rd June, the feast of Corpus Christi. In the Hospital chapel, which stands to this very day, Bernadette made her first acquaintance with Jesus under the form of the host. As yet she had not acquired much religious knowledge. Her religious exam, prior to her taking first Communion, had shown her to be ill at ease with the abstract formulas of the catechism. Although it could have been said that she knew nothing, one felt that in fact she knew it all. After all, wasn't it she who had, that very spring, the best catechism teacher ever ?

« Everything seems to be developing in her in the most amazing way », wrote Father Peyramale to his Bishop that same evening. When a friend asked Bernadette :

« What makes you happier, the Communion or the Apparitions ? she answered : - « The two things go together, but they cannot be compared. I was happy with both ». Bernadette's answers never cease to surprise !

« I thank you, Father », Jesus once said, « for having revealed these things to the poor and the humble ».

A page from Jacomet's notebook | Chapel where Bernadette made her first communion

Lourdes - scene of unrest

Because of the antics of false visionaries and other troublemakers at the Grotto, Lourdes was in a frenzied state of unrest. The clergy watched and waited hoping for some decision from the Bishop on the matter. Mgr Laurence, a cool character, not normally given to rush matters, abruptly intervened. In a letter, written on July 9th, he denounced the abuses that were taking place but made no mention of Bernadette. Father Peyramale supported the Bishop's condemnation and followed his orders.

The civil authorities were also under pressure. While it was clear that neither Bernadette nor the clergy had anything to do with the unrest, nevertheless, the Prefect, Imperial Prosecutor and Police Commissioner were all agreed that the Massabielle phenomenon had to stop. On the pretext that the water from the Grotto might be dangerous, the Grotto was declared out of bounds and barricaded. Verbal reprimands from the police rained down on anyone who tried to break in. Workmen from Lourdes, forced by the police to erect barricades by day, demolished them by night. An event that was to happen three times !

The last Apparition : July 16th : Obedient to the orders of the Bishop and the laws imposed by the civil authorities, Bernadette had been living in peaceful obscurity far from the feverish unrest, when suddenly, on the feast of Our Lady of Mount Carmel, she felt drawn once more to Masssabielle.

The powerful call that she could never resist led her across the Gave to the far side of the meadow (where the Carmelite convent is now situated). « I only saw the Virgin and she was more beautiful than ever. » The two friends quietly made their goodbyes amid the silent, fervent crowd.

For Bernadette life continued, simply and fervently, in the poverty of the old gaol where she lived. It was only in September that they were able to leave this miserable hovel, although it was almost another full year before François Soubirous recovered his work and his dignity as a master miller.

Having travelled the path of « Darkness and Light », Lourdes was now launched on the seas of history. On July 28th, Mgr Laurence appointed a commission to investigate the entire affair. For over three years this commission was to work, study and enquire. After Bernadette was officially questioned on November 17th, every witness was interrogated and countless reports made. Inexplicable cures were examined. A team of doctors, under the supervision of the eminent Professor Vergez of the Faculty of Medicine of Montpellier, confirmed thirty five cases of inexplicable healing. It was this factor, together with the undoubted credibility of Bernadette herself, that finally convinced the Bishop to declare, in a Pastoral Letter dated January 18th 1862, that « truly, the Virgin did appear to Bernadette ».

Meanwhile, under pressure from the many believers who argued that harsh police measures only added to the sources of unrest, the Emperor Napoleon III intervened. Anxious not to displease the local populace he ordered the barricades to be removed from the Grotto.

Peace and order now restored, the Grotto of Apparitions was soon to become, within the space of three years, the place of prayer and contemplation that it continues to be today.

BERNADETTE
✠
LOVRDES
✠1858✠

« Now I'm just like everybody else »

From the ecstatic wonder that had filled her heart at Massabielle, Bernadette now set out to live her life in the simple fidelity of a simple faith just « like everybody else ».

And remarkably, she succeeded. She avoided playing the role of a celebrity as much as she avoided that danger of being caught up in herself that the wonderful inner experiences of the Apparitions could have provoked. And she succeeded in this in spite of constant bad health, enduring family problems, and the incessant harassment of journalists and curiosity seekers.

At least the filthy « Cachot » was at last left behind. A move to the Gras mill became for Bernadette almost like a return to childhood and her joy was complete as she saw her beloved father recover his work and his dignity as a master miller.

In response to the questions of Azun de Bernatas, a journalist this is how her mother described what Bernadette was living then :

« She attends school run by the Sisters of Nevers, and seems to be quite happy.

Since February 11th her health has got worse. Her stomach swells at times to such an extent that she can no longer button her dress ; her coughing becomes more frequent and troublesome while this swelling lasts making her suffer for weeks on end, leaving her then returning a little later on.

During her moments of better health, or when she suffers less, she occupies herself with household chores. As she's the eldest of the family, she helps me look after her brothers and sisters and with the housework.

She wanted to fast last Lent but we had to forbid her from doing it. »

Bernadette was to remain with her family for two years. A brother was born on September 10th 1859. This was Louise's seventh child, and she had already lost two as babies. Bernadette became the godmother of little Pierre and always remained extremely conscious of her responsibility.

Plans were made to take her from the family and entrust her to the care of the nuns where she could continue her education, and where she might be better protected from the incessant harassment of visitors who had begun to disrupt her daily life and that of the family : « Oh, I understand you well enough, Reverend Father, but I love my father and mother so much », was Bernadette's reply to Father Peyramale who was mainly responsible for the whole idea. A friendly neighbour, Augustine Tardhivail, lovingly helped her in her efforts to learn to read, write and speak French. She never became brilliant at them, but she faced her difficulties with courage and eventually was able to render an ever clearer account of the Apparitions.

Important Bishops, from Soissons and Montpellier, as well as Veuillot, a famous reporter from the newspaper l'Univers, all came to question her. All were astonished by her simplicity, her coherence and her strength of character. The visiting Bishops harassed Mgr Laurence, the Bishop of Tarbes : « He cannot just stand idly by. This amazing affair must be investigated. » Veuillot published a sensational account in his paper. When asked if she was affected by this, Bernadette simply replied : « I hardly know how to read ».

On February 5th 1860, Bernadette was confirmed by Mgr Laurence himself. It was the first time that the Bishop of the diocese had met her, and this two years after the Apparitions.

Meanwhile the Church commission, organised since the summer of the Apparitions, worked hard. Bernadette was questioned at the Grotto on November 17th. The members of the commission were favourably impressed but wanted time to reflect, observe and study.

Bernadette at the Hospice

Bernadette was now 16 years old. Realising her position had become impossible, she decided, with the help of her parents, to accept the proposal put forward by Fr Peyramale and Lacadé the Mayor to enter the hospice run by the Sisters of Nevers. Entering the hospice, on July 15th 1860, as a sick person in need, she pursued her studies at the hospice school and helped the Sisters in their work.

Having only agreed to enter the hospice on the firm promise that she would be « free to go and visit her parents », Bernadette proved more than capable of defending this clause in her contract. Throughout her life she played the role of the eldest sister in a firm yet tender way. Nothing would ever separate her from her roots and from her oneness with those she loved.

Indeed, on entering the hospice, she had insisted on being placed in the « 2nd » class, reserved to boarders of modest means. Again, in the light of the Gospel, she demonstrated her intent to remain poor and with the poor.

« At breaks she is the life and soul of the party. Always cheerful, she joins in games with the younger classes, although she gets out of breath », observed the nuns. She was entrusted with the younger children immediately. Her small stature was a definite asset in this endeavour and children took to her easily.

Never given to playing « the little model Saint », Bernadette lived her youth to the full with all its qualities and all its defects.

There was the story of how one day she threw her shœ into the « forbidden » garden and then got her friend Julie Garros to bring it back and some strawberries with it !

On another occasion, Sister Victorine was surprised to see that Bernadette entertained fancies about her dress. One day she found her trying to « widen her skirt » after the fashion of the « crinolines » worn by the well-to-do girls and considered as « diabolical » by the clergy. Another time she tried to make a « bust » for herself with bits of wood.

Some were shocked by these antics. But they were just amusing incidents in the life of a teenager. Indeed the absence of such behaviour would have been more disturbing.

And yet underneath all this lively, playful behaviour, deeper currents of thought and reflection began to form in her heart.

The Hospice

Bernadette and the Superior of the Hospice

« Bernadette, a vocation like everybody else »

The moving book by Dom Bernard Billet describes so well the long and careful deliberations that took place in the development of Bernadette's vocation.

Before the end of the Apparitions, Bernadette firmly declared her intention to Lacadé the Mayor, that she « wanted to be a nun ». Even then her heart chose to give the greatest love possible. But it was to take her all of six years of thought, prayer and searching reflection until, at the age of twenty, she annouced her decision.

Suggestions and invitations as to whom she should join came from all quarters and from various convents. Would she become a contemplative at the « Bernardine » convent of Anglet, founded by Father Cestac the saviour of prostitutes and whose holiness was renowned throughout the region ?

Or would she be a Carmelite like Augustine Tardhivail, her teacher, whose bad health had kept her from returning to the Carmelite convent at Bagnères ?

The Sisters of the Cross of Bétharram would have liked to take her in. She once tried putting on the quaint « cornette », the strange headdress, worn by them, and exclaimed : « I'll never wear this silly thing ! »

The Sisters of Saint Vincent de Paul had no more success when they tried the same thing. Dressing Bernadette in their costume topped by another famous headgear they said to the young girl : « This will give you your vocation Bernadette. »

« Oh no, exactly the opposite », was the firm reply.

The only ones never to speak to her of a vocation, this being one of their rules, were the Sisters of Nevers with whom she lived and worked every day. With them she applied herself not only to helping at school but also with the chores at the hospice.

It was there at the hospice that Bernadette welcomed « the drunkard » of Lourdes, a poor old woman who one day having drunk too much, fell, hurt herself badly and needed treatment. After having tended her wounds, Bernadette kissed her, laughing and saying, « from now on you mustn't take so many swigs ».

Once Bernadette confided to her friend Jeanne Védère : « I love the poor a lot and I like taking care of the sick ; I'll stay with the Sisters of Nevers. They gave me a sick person to take care of and when I'm feeling well, nobody else takes care of him but me. I'll stay there with them. »

To stay there and serve, why not ? But in order to become one of this distinguished congregation of teachers, she needed an education, good health, and a dowry.

When the proposal to enter the Convent of Nevers without having to pay was made to her by Mgr Forcade, the Bishop of Nevers, who visited Lourdes in September of 1863, Bernadette replied with moving simplicity : « But the girls you take in without a dowry are skillful and clever and are well worth the trouble... I don't know anything, I'm a good for nothing. »

Bernadette nevertheless turned over the Bishop's proposal in her mind, a proposal far more important than the commotion taking place around her, as photographers fought for permission from the nuns and from the Bishop to take her portrait. As they urged her to mime ecstatic poses « just like when the Lady was there », Bernadette, wrapped up in more important thoughts and against the whole idea, dryly replied that « the Lady isn't there anymore ».

« They want to show me off like cattle at a fair » was her comment to the indiscreet curiosity which harassed her from all sides. She laughed at the portraits of her that were being sold for a few sous : « That's about all I'm worth », she said.

Bernadette - a true character

For Bernadette the most painful thing was to be treated as a saint. She never encouraged the image of the « mystical » saint, and was opposed to every artifical posture of piety that might have suggested such an idea. She was totally natural. Father Ravier, who made a deep study of her psychology, described her in the following way :

« This stubborn Bigourdane girl is energetic, courageous, combative, and knows what she wants till the bitter end, not letting the strongest arguments trip her up, nor the most thundrous threats bend her will ; she has nothing in common with a « perfect little saint » : this is the real Bernadette.

Her acute sensitivity is balanced by a rare strength of character. Happily so, because already her « touchiness », (as it was later to be called at the Convent and by Bernadette herself), her lively reactions to people, events and things, were starting to make themselves felt ».

All her life she strove to temper her single-minded character : « I am said to be head-strong and that makes me ashamed », she humbly said.

Meanwhile, as the story of the Apparitions deepened, Bernadette's importance increased. Now she was to become the centre of attention in the affair of the statue at the Grotto.

The rich Latour sisters of Lyon commissioned Fabish, the most famous sculptor of the time, to carve a Carrara marble statue depicting the Apparitions. The artist came to see Bernadette so that she could describe the vision to him, and was impressed. But more caught up in his own ideals of grandeur and his « academic outlook », he was to sculpt a

great Lady who bore no resemblance whatsœver to the « little lady », so full of life and kindness, that Bernadette could never forget. When, one evening, the work was presented to Bernadette, Fabish was showered in compliments and praise by the adults present but he saw in the eyes of this child that he had failed. « No, she wasn't like that », declared Bernadette. Fabish was later to say that these words were « the greatest sorrow of his artistic life ».

The statue of the Apparitions

The decision - April 4th 1864

The statue was nevertheless placed in the recess of the rock of Massabielle and solemnly blessed. Bernadette was absent on this day of triumph for the Grotto. The « pig-sty » had now become a holy place where a huge procession took place in all pomp and ceremony with its colourful banners, its thousands of pilgrims, and the once hostile authorities in attendance with the Bishop, Mgr Laurence, and all his clergy.

Far from the enthusiastic crowd Bernadette remained at the Hospice and on that same day told her Mother Superior, Sister Alexandrine, of the decision she had made :

« Now I know, my dear Mother, where I must become a nun. »

« Where then, my child ? »

« At your Convent, Mother. »

« Well then, we'll speak to his Excellency. »

Two years were to go by before the decision became reality.

Firstly, Bernadette's already fragile health took a serious turn for the worse at the end of the year and she was still in bed by February 1865. Then her little brother Justin died at the age of ten. The malnutrition of years of misery was dearly paid for by the Soubirous. Bernadette was at her mother's side during this time of sorrow, the third child Louise had lost at a tender age.

The following year, on April 28th 1866, Bernadette announced her departure. She was then 22 years old.

Mgr Laurence delayed the departure for a few weeks wanting her to attend, on May 9th, the inauguration of the Crypt that had been solidly built on the rock of Massabielle. François Soubirous had worked as a navvy on this project. Above the Crypt, the Upper Basilica, the « chapel » the Lady had asked for, was soon to follow. Bernadette felt she could now leave, her message being engraved on the very stone, the very countryside of Lourdes.

The building site of the crypt and the 1st official procession (4/4/1864) for the inauguration of the Statue

18 Goodbye to Lourdes

On the evening of **July 3ʳᵈ 1866**, everyone gathered at the Lacadé mill (the present day Maison Paternelle) for the last meal together.

The next morning, her father and mother with her two aunts, Bernarde and Basile, went to the hospice for the last goodbye. Bernadette, carrying a coarse gaudy linen bag and big umbrella, put on a brave face in the midst of the general sorrow and tried to comfort everyone. « We were all in tears », said Pierre, Bernadette's godson now aged 6.

« You are very good to cry, but I can't stay forever », she said with firmness.

She had by then overcome the sorrow which had overwhelmed her the day before when she had bid farewell at the Grotto.

« The Grotto was my heaven » she was to say.

A coach took her to the station, the train moved out, the mountains faded behind her in the distance. Goodbye Lourdes.

Bernadette was never again to see her beautiful countryside nor the Grotto. One day she even said, « When I die people will want to take my body back to Lourdes. They will be unable to ». Her mission now continues, elsewhere.

Documents of the time

A few photographs remain, taken in haste at the last moment by Viron, a Lourdes photographer : Bernadette with her family, and also by Billard-Perrin :
Bernadette among the nuns.
Bernadette among the " *Children of Mary* ".

Bernadette with the nuns

Bernadette becomes a nun

On July 7th, late at night, after a tiring two day journey, in the company of two nuns and two fellow postulants, Bernadette arrived at the immense convent that housed the « Sisters of Charity and Christian Learning of Nevers ». In the great silence of the darkened cloister, exhausted, they went off to bed immediately.

On the following day Bernadette was shown around the convent. Dressed for the very last time in the old Pyrenean fashion with her little white hood, she was made to recount the story of Lourdes before all 300 nuns who lived there. It was the last time she was to speak publicly of the Apparitions.

Forbidden ever to broach the subject again, she donned the little pleated cap and dress of the postulant and disappeared into the anonymity of the huge community.

« I came here to hide », she once said. When any personal praise was given to her for the Apparitions, (that still continued to capture world interest and attract ever increasing crowds to Lourdes), she would reply quite simply :

« I am just a broom in the hands of the Virgin Mary. What do you do with a broom when you have finished using it ? You put it away behind the door. That's my place and that's where I'm staying. »

On July 29th, Bernadette donned the religious habit and received the name of Sister Marie-Bernard. To protect her from the harassment of the curious, it was decided that she should stay at the Mother House of Nevers. In spite of her desire to devote herself elsewhere, she quietly accepted the decision. Such was her discretion and unassuming manner, that a newly arrived novice, upon discovering the identity of the quiet nun with whom she had been speaking, exclaimed :

« So that's Bernadette, is it ? », and Bernadette replied laughing, « Yes, I'm afraid it is ».

On August 15th she was again confined to bed sick. Between attacks of asthma she sang « in Pyrenean dialect », and laughed to see that her companions understood nothing. Even the Holy Virgin understood the dialect of Lourdes !

On October 25th the Bishop was alerted. Bernadette seemed on the point of death. Arriving in the middle of the night, he received her vows, and administered extreme unction, as the sacrament of the sick was then called.

She recovered and said jokingly : « The Good God didn't want me... » She rejoiced at having received the veil and crucifix just like the other nuns. They were a token of belonging and filled her with peace and joy : « Now they can't get rid of me », she said.

On December 8th Bernadette was shocked to learn of the death of her mother. On

Portrait Authentique
DE MA
Sœur Bernadette
J.M. Stchérou

The Nun Marie-Bernard

the feast of the Immaculate Conception, at the age of 41, Louise Soubirous died, worn out by a life of hard work, poverty and by the death of five young children. Bernadette's sorrow was deep and Lourdes so far away. It was to Our Lady of the Waters, the smiling Virgin at the bottom of the convent garden, that Bernadette went to pour out her heart. She asked Our Lady to be her mother from then on as her life continued its quiet and courageous course.

Her simplicity and joyful spontaneous character amazed everyone. One day, on May 16th 1867, a new arrival, Miss Dalias de Lectoure, tried to find out who the « Visionary of Lourdes » was. It is interesting to read what she wrote to her family :

« No one was willing to answer my questions and especially this pretty charming girl, the prettiest of the whole group. She was so childlike, alive spontaneous and with such a simplicity that I never imagined her to be the one... »

Bernadette's mother

When someone did point out Bernadette, the young lady exclaimed : « That one ! », and Bernadette offering her hand said : « But yes... only that, nothing more ».

On **July 30th 1867**, a year after her entrance, Bernadette renewed her religious profession taken so suddenly the previous autumn when it was thought she was dying. Her old touchiness surfaced once more. « Like everybody else » she wanted to work for the Church in some place other than Nevers, but it was judged prudent that she remain within the protecting walls of the Mother house. « She is good for nothing », publicly proclaimed the Mother General. « I warned you at Lourdes that I was good for nothing », replied Bernadette to the Bishop of Nevers who had encouraged her to join this congregation. « Well then », concluded the Bishop, « I give you the job of prayer ».

Bernadette never forgot this mission. Was it not the first and deep discovery she had made at the Grotto ? Prayer was an intimate relationship with « the other world », already present in her. An intercession for « this world » where so many « poor sinners » do not know that « God weeps for our sins like a mother ».

But this prayer is neither an inward withdrawal nor escape. Bernadette was now to show what she was capable of.

Bernadette as a nurse

« We could keep her out of charity at the Mother house and give her some kind of work in the infirmary, even if it is just cleaning and preparing drinks for the sick. As she is always ill, this is just the job for her. » It was with these words of the Mother General that Bernadette, without much education and no qualification, began work as the main nurse of the great house.

We still have her nurse's notebook where she wrote down the amounts needed to make up potions according to the new system of weights and measures introduced at the time. Quietly and intelligently this makeshift nurse coped admirably with her responsibilities and won the complete confidence of the house Doctor. When an anticlerical campaign was launched against Lourdes, stating that Bernadette, the famous visionary, was nothing more than an idiot hidden away in an Ursuline convent at Nevers, Dr Robert Saint Cyr, chairman of the Society of Doctors of Nièvre, insisted on publishing the following declaration :

« Here is a nurse who carries out her task to perfection. Small and puny, she is 27 years old. With her calm and gentle nature, she cares for her patients intelligently and omits nothing from the prescriptions given her. She also exercises great authority and, as far as I am concerned, has my entire confidence » (September 3rd 1872).

Bernadette showed her intelligence in many different ways. Handicapped by her bad start at school, she was never brilliant at spelling, although she wrote many letters. She was, however, very skillful with her hands and embroidered many beautiful things. The Museum of Lourdes displays a lace alb made entirely by herself.

The Saint-Gildard Convent

Her finely attuned psychology did wonders for her distressed companions. It became customary to send her all those in need of peace and fresh courage. A nurse of the heart as well as the body, she had an ability to console born of personal suffering.

With France and Prussia declaring war in 1870, and the Prussian invasion imminent, Bernadette comforted those around her. When cannons were installed in the convent courtyard, which dominated the plain of Nevers, she wrote to her father : « I could do without the Prussians, but I'm not afraid of them. God is everywhere, even among the Prussians ».

When she learnt that warring partisans had burnt down the Tuileries, an ancient Parisian residence of the Kings of France, an act that maddened the community, Bernadette astonishingly commented : « Don't worry about it, the buildings needed repainting and God just used his brush. » As a clear-headed common girl she was unimpressed by the Imperial Court and all its brilliant luxury, and saw clearly the misery into which the poor were led by the indifference of the great.

In this 19th century, the age of « enlightenment », intoxicated with scientific and technical discoveries, enamoured with economic expansion, once again, the poor had been forgotten.

« Make yourselves rich », a Minister exclaimed at the French National Assembly. « Workers of the world, unite », wrote Karl Marx in 1848. New wars, new revolutions were being prepared...

Convent of Nevers, military hospital

France was invaded by the Prussians. The Superior General placed the convent at the disposal of the war department.

The nuns were evacuated except for a little group including Bernadette who was in charge of the infirmary.

Sick and wounded soldiers filled the house. A diary kept by the Superior contains a painful account of the sicknesses and deaths.

One can only imagine the immense suffering and anguish when confronted with terrible wounds from the battlefields in an era so limited in the ways of medicine and surgery.

Bernadette and her companions worked unceasingly. The film producer, Jean Delannoy, in his last film « Bernadette's Passion », did not hesitate to show us an unprecedented scene : Bernadette attending to a wounded person during one of these appalling surgical operations.

The poor little asthmatic had such a concern for the sick and did all she could to tend to the wounds of body and heart.

Bernadette's prayer books

Bernadette's rosary

The difficult ascent

The father Bernadette loved so much, François Soubirous, died on March 4th 1871. Memories flooded Bernadette's heart ; memories of the mill of happiness and the sweet smell of flour, and of a father unjustly imprisoned during the years of their misfortune. When she had been living in exile at Bartrès, he was the one who had come to cheer her up ; when threatened by the Police Commissioner, he was the one who had come to her defence. Now the father to whom she was the firstborn and the favourite child, was no more.

Bernadette did not hide her sorrow : « My tears are joined with yours », she wrote to her sister Marie, « let us bear and embrace this cross ».

From 1874 onwards sickness and suffering became the very substance of Bernadette's life. « My job is to be sick », was the comment she made, as she pondered her painful condition in the light of God's providence. From April to June she was bedridden. Worn out by asthma, tuberculosis now invaded her lungs. She suffered terribly as her choking fits increased, and decay of the bones of her knee worsened.

In early November 1878 she was taken to Saint Croix, a room used as an infirmary for the professed religious. She was never to leave it alive. On December 11th she took up permanent residence in her « white chapel » as she called her big curtained bed. She kept herself busy painting or embroidering hearts and said jokingly : « No one can say that Sister Marie-Bernard is heartless ! ». She also embroidered crosses surrounded by a crown of thorns with the inscription « God is Love », the motto of the Sisters of Nevers that is engraved on the St-Gildard convent.

Bernadette's father

Holy-water font in the chapel of St Gildard

The Statue of Bernadette

52

In all her sick-bed activities, with the gay remarks that accompanied them, Bernadette made it quite clear that she had no unhealthy preoccupation with suffering. « I pray to Saint Bernard (her Patron Saint) but I don't imitate him. He liked suffering and I avoid it as much as I can. »

For Bernadette suffering only had meaning in relation to love. Since her life at Lourdes, she had faithfully meditated on the Way of the Cross. At Nevers she even kept a printed copy of the Way of the Cross on her death-bed. It was Christ's passion for sinners that enlightened all she had to endure. « Everything really began for her at Lourdes at the 9th Apparition », affirmed Father Ravier who carried out a lengthy study of Bernadette's religious psychology. Although he reveals in his writings that « the Saints do not tell it all », his profound analysis leads us to see that the discovery of the world of sinners, on the days she discovered the muddy spring, had opened to Bernadette a way of compassion that she lived in the depths of her heart. The « man of sorrows », the victim for sinners, lived in her prayer. « If only sinners knew » she sighed one day.

Father Peyramale, now Monsignor Peyramale, the « priest of the Apparitions » was very dear to Bernadette's heart. With the confrontations of the past well and truly forgotten, he became the vigorous defender of Bernadette's honour. « Before touching a hair on her head they will have to step over my dead body », he would say if anyone tried to suggest that the visionary was a mad woman in need of lock-ing up. From the time of his belief in the Apparitions he had always supported Berna-dette. He wore himself out, and even ruined his family financially in his zeal to build a Church worthy of a town that was growing daily with the arrival of more and more pil-grims.

Bernadette was told of the priest's death - on September 8th 1877 - and had one more sorrow to add to her own great suffering.

Worried about her family, she suffered for her sister Toinette who had lost one child after another, suffered in fear that her bro-thers might take the wrong direction in life, and suffered to see so much money pouring into Lourdes because of the pilgrims : « If only they wouldn't get rich. Tell them not to get rich », she implored a passing priest on his way to Lourdes to visit her family.

And her suffering continued with the inces-sant demands of people wanting to see her. To journalists who fought for her approval to write the story of Lourdes, she said « what-ever has to be written, the shorter the better ».

When she was called to the visiting room « she almost had to be dragged there », and reminded all and sundry of the promise made, to keep her hidden in the far off convent. Her feelings were not for the curious, but for the « poor sinners, who were our brothers ».

The last questions and demands of that valuable and thorough historian Father Cros, wore her out. Although she could say « I am happier on my bed of pain with my crucifix, than a queen upon her throne » her passion and suffering were immense. Soon even her memory abandoned her. « She remembers nothing » said the Superior.

The Passion of Bernadette

Even towards the last, with what little strength remained, Bernadette still managed the occasional joke. Like the time when she saw the nun taking care of her not get any sleep and said : « I don't want this nun to watch over me any more... I want sleeping nuns. » But the brave courage and cheerful remarks diminished more and more as her suffering began to reach its climax : « How the end takes so long to come », she said in agony.

« Worn out and weary in her suffering, she had all wasted away », wrote Father Cros. « She was subjected », commented Father Fèbre, the chaplain who visited and faithfully supported her throughout her terrible illnesses, « to such torment of bone decay for two years that her poor body became a receptacle for all the suffering in the world ».

« The Passion », Bernadette had once said, « touches me more when I read it than when someone explains it to me ». Now her very agony mirrored the Passion of Jesus to whom she had given all her love and all her life. Hers was not the stoic death of some iron-willed hero, but of one dying, like her master before her, in an agony of love.

« Look amongst your drugs... find something to strengthen me. I feel so weak. I can't breathe. Give me strong vinegar to smell ».

Was Jesus on the Cross not given vinegar to drink ?

As memories of her chidhood flitted through her mind Bernadette softly murmured : « I am crushed like a grain of wheat ».

Days and nights went by. On the last day she had her crucifix laid upon her heart. All she saw was HIM. « You are on the Cross », said a nun. « My Jesus ! Oh! How much I love you », was Bernadette's only answer on that Easter Wednesday. Twenty one years before, the flame of her candle had licked her hands for a long time without burning her. The time had now come to pass into that other world where all suffering ends and where « God will wipe away every tear from our eyes ».

Towards three o'clock in the afternoon, the time of Christ's own death, Bernadette, in an expression of pain, stretched out her arms and gave out the loud cry : « My God ! » She then joined in prayer with her companions and twice repeated : « Holy Mary, Mother of God, pray for me a poor sinner. » Even her last prayer reflected her love and solidarity with the « poor sinners » for whom she had sacrificed so much.

She looked intently at a nun who had promised to « help her give thanks to the Blessed Virgin right up to the very end », and said to her « if you would help me ». She made a sign for something to drink. She then took a few sips, lowered her head and gently delivered up her spirit.

Crucifix given to her on becoming a nun

The body of Bernadette

Bernadette died at the age of 35 on Wednesday April 16th 1879.

The news spread rapidly. Crowds flocked to the St-Gildard Convent, from Nevers itself, and from the surrounding regions. Everyone wanted to see and venerate the remains of the woman who, thirteen years earlier, had come here « to hide » and who believed she would be forgotten.

But crowds of people had kept a place in their hearts for the little girl from Lourdes.

An endless procession of people filed past to venerate her. Newspapers of the period describe the fervour and emotion of these crowds, crowds so great that permission to expose the body for three days had to be requested from the civil authorities.

The writer Zola reports that « Lasserre saw her dead. He said she was very beautiful[1] ».

On April 19th the body was « placed in a double coffin of lead and oak and sealed in the presence of witnesses who signed the report ». Inspector Decraine and policemen Saget and Moyen signed this declaration. The body was buried in the vault of a little chapel in the garden that was dedicated to St-Joseph. « My Father St-Joseph » Bernadette used to say.

Did everything end here ?

The answer is no, because in the course of time, far from fading away, the memory of Bernadette grew greater and greater. Miracles were attributed to her. More and more was said and written about the saintliness of this girl who just wanted to be « like everybody else ».

---

1 : Laurentin : « The life of Bernadette ».

The first exhumation

In 1909, 30 years after her death, the « Process of Canonisation » or more simply the investigation into the saintliness of Bernadette, demanded a « recognition of the body ».

On September 9th that year, a group of eminent personalities gathered in the garden of the Nevers convent. Present were the Bishop of Nevers, several Church dignitaries, a number of Superiors from the Convent, two forensic pathologists, Drs. Jourdan and Davin, the Mayor of Nevers and his first officer to assist him with the formalities.

From the report drawn up by the authorised doctors we note the following matters of interest :

« We perceived no odour at all. - The body was covered in the habit of her Order which was damp. Only the face, hands and forearms were uncovered.

The head was bent to the left and the face was of a dull white hue ; the skin adhering to the muscles and the muscles fixed to the bones. - Sunken eyelids covered her eyes. - The eyebrows were stuck to the arch of the brow and adhered to the skin as did the eyelashes on the upper right eyelid. - The nose was parchmentlike and sharp. - The mouth was slightly open displaying the teeth still attached to the gums. - The hands, crossed on the chest, were perfectly preserved with their nails, and still carried a rosary corroded by rust. - The outline of the veins could be seen on the forearm. »

Second exhumation

In 1913, Rome authorised the continuation of the Process for the Beatification and Canonisation of Bernadette. The 1914-18 war put a stop to everything.

On April 3rd 1919, a second recognition of the body took place in the presence of the Bishop, Mgr Chatelus, the Commissioner of

Police, representatives of the municipality and of the Church tribunal. Two doctors, Dr. Talon and Dr. Comte, both forensic experts, were given the task of examining the body.

Each made out his report in a separate office at the scene of the examination. Each of the texts states almost the same things and are in complete agreement with the medical reports written ten years earlier, at the first exhumation.

Third exhumation

In 1923 the Pope proclaimed « as heroic » the virtues of Bernadette. She was about to become a Saint.

In 1925, on April 18th, 46 years after her death, her body was again examined. With the Bishop of Nevers and members of the Church tribunal, stood Mabille, the Police Commissionner, Mr Bruneton representing the Mayor of Nevers and the two medical experts, Dr. Toulon and Dr. Comte the surgeon. This is how the latter expressed what particularly captured his attention :

« What struck me in this examination was, of course, the state of perfect preservation of the skeleton, the tendons, the ligaments and the skin, the suppleness and tone of the muscles, and above all the most unexpected condition of the liver after 46 years. It seems that this essentially delicate and soft organ should have decomposed rapidly or calcified and become hard, but upon cutting it, it was of a soft, almost normal consistency. I let those present observe this and told them that in my opinion the phenomenon did not seem to be of the natural order. »

On July 18th the body was placed in a glass reliquary where it can be seen to this very day on entering the chapel of the Convent of the Sisters of Nevers.

The Church does not claim this extraordinary preservation of the body to be a miracle in the strict sense of the word. In spite of the scientifically inexplicable facts involved, the phenomenon may one day be explained. But can we not see in this a sign from Bernadette - a last wink of the eye ?

She, whose life so transparently mirrored the Gospels, whose life experienced poverty and exhaustion, like Jesus himself did right to his death on the Cross, now rests peacefully like a child who will one day awaken from sleep. It is the message of eternal life, that the Gospels and Bernadette still speak of.

A relic taken from Bernadette's body is kept in a crafted reliquary in Lourdes and is carried in procession on special feast days.

Facsimile of Dr Talon's report

Are there still miracles at Lourdes ?

Even before the end of the Apparitions the astonishing news of extraordinary healings was widespread.

On March 1st 1858, Catherine Latapie Chouat, whose arm was paralysed after an accident, suddenly was healed as she soaked it in the Spring discovered by Bernadette on February 25th.

Above all there was Louis Borriette, the Quarryman and stone-cutter. He was caught in a mine explosion 20 years earlier. His brother Joseph, next to him, had been killed outright. Louis had been atrociously wounded and had lost an eye. Suddenly in March 1858, he regained his sight when his son brought him a little water from the Grotto with which to bathe his lost eye.

Out of 35 cases presented to the Commision of Inquiry set up to investigate the events of the Apparitions these were 2 of the 7 which were recognised as miraculous. The work of investigation and medical observation was at that time entrusted to Professor Vergez of the faculty of medecine at Montpellier.

Since then the careful scrutiny of healings has been refined over the years and has become more organised and perfected. The Medical Bureau of Lourdes considers all declarations of healing and whether or not they merit further study and serious investigation.

In the offices of the Medical Bureau located on the Esplanade, the photos of those who have been cured can be seen together with a brief summary of their medical history. Any doctor, whatever his or her beliefs may be, or whether a believer or not, has access to the medical files of Lourdes. 15,000 doctors from all over the world belong to the International Medical Association of Lourdes. When an alledged cure is received by the Medical Bureau it is sent to the International Medical Commission of Lourdes where 30 or so specialists make an in-depth study of the case in question. Up to the present day some 2,500 inexplicable healings have been considered. This is the **work of the doctors.**

The religious authority, the Bishop of the person « recognised as healed in an inexplicable way » by the International Medical Commission, then undertakes an inquiry to determine whether or not this healing can be declared as the **work of God**, that is a miracle. This is the **work of the Church.**

Up to the present the Church has declared 65 miracles due to the action of God through the intercession of Our Lady of Lourdes.

The last recognised miracle, after 12 years of medical and religious inquiry, was declared on June 28th 1989. The person concerned was Delizia Cirolli who at the age of 11 had a cancerous tumour and who was healed at Lourdes in 1976. Now married and known as Mrs. Costa she continues to come to Lourdes as a nurse.

Francis PASCAL (47436)
02/08/1938 : guérie de SICILE & de Para-
plégie Etague post-ménin-
gitique
02/09/1946 & 12/07/19.. : guérie
21/06/1949 : Miracle n°45 (Aix-en-Provence).

Gabrielle CLAUZEL (46006)
15/08/1943 : guérie de Spondylose rhéma-
tismale.
19/02/1945 : constatation de la guérison
19/03/1948 : confirmation de la guérison
14/05/1948 : Miracle n°46 (Oran).

Yvonne FOURNIER (40619)
19/08/1945 : guérie de Syndrome catonevro-
progressif post-traumatique
19/08/1950 : constatation de la guérison
14/11/1953 : confirmation par le Comité
Médical National de Lourdes
(Facial).

Mme Rose MARTIN - née BORGIA (42058)
03/07/1947 : guérie de Néoplasme d'un
cancer du col opéré.
03/07/1946 : constatation de la guérison
29/08/1949 : confirmation par le Comité
Médical National de Lourdes
19/09/19..

Mme Jeanne
02/06/19.

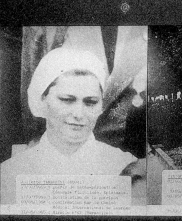

(65534)
05/0. & 07/10/1964 : guérie de
Hémiplégie D.. et de porteur..
constatation de la guérison
confirmation par le Comité
international de Lourdes
Miracle n°59 (Rennes).

Mme Ginette NOUVEL - née FABRE (49061)
21/05/1954 : guérie de Maladie de Budd-Chiari
27/07/1960 : constatation de la guérison
13/04/1961 : confirmation par le Comité Médical International de Lourdes
31/05/1963 : Miracle n°60 (Albi).

Elisa ALOI (59008)
05/06/1958 : guérie de Tuberculose osté-
articulaire multiple et
fistulisée
23/05/1961 : confirmation par le Comité
Médical International de
Lourdes
26/05/1965 : Miracle n°61 (Messine).

Juliette TAMBURINI (60045)
17/07/1959 : guérie de Ostéo-périostite
Hémorragie fistulisée. Epistaxis.
09/06/1961 : constatation de la guérison
09/05/1964 : confirmation par le Comité
Médical International de Lourdes
11/05/1965 : Miracle n°62 (Marseille).

Vittorio MICHELI
01/06/1963 :
07/05/1967 : const
03/09/1971 : confi
Médi
26/05/1976 : Mira

Signorina Delizia CIROLLI,   PATERNO (Sicile)

vers Noël 1976 : guérison d'une Tumeur
d'Ewing (tibia droit)

8/07/1980 : certification par le Bureau
Médical

6/09/1982 : confirmation par le Comité
Médical International de Lourdes

③

④

The pilgrim's way

Just like millions of your contemporaries, you have left everything behind. Today nobody waits for you, neither at the factory, nor at the office, nor the workshop. There is no shopping to be done, no housework waiting. Free from everything, free for the essential, you are ready to take the pilgrim's way.

We come from the four corners of the Earth

1 - 2 : At the station « Here we are at last »

3 : The sick disembark at the airport

4 : The basilicas and Pyrenees

Map of the Shrine

1 ● Grotto

2 ● Baths

3 ● Invalids' Way of the Cross

4 ● Meadow

5 ● Our Lady's hospital care centre

6 ● Drinking fountains

7 ● Rosary Basilica

8 ● Medical Bureau - Offices of Our Lady's *Hospitalité*

9 ● Pastoral Care Centre

10 ● Esplanade Chapels

11 ● Crypt

12 ● Upper Basilica (of the Immaculate Conception)

13 ● Way of the Cross

14 ● Chapel of Reconciliation

15 ● Chaplaincy

16 ● Saint Peter's reception office

Pilgrimage reception office

Reception - Information

Statue of the Crowned Virgin

The former hospital care centre of Our Lady

Saint Joseph's Church

Saint Pius X Underground Basilica

Shrine Museum

Notre-Dame Hall

25 ● Pavilions - diverse Church movements and groups

26 ● Vizens Bridge

27 ● Pax Christi Youth Centre

28 ● Saint Frai's hospital care centre

29 ● Saint Peter's

30 ● Youth Camp

31 ● Saint Bernadette's Church

« Tourists, individuals »

There are smiling multi-lingual hostesses from many countries, waiting to give you the information you require and to show you with slides and recordings in 80 languages the « Message of Lourdes ».

Welcome.

◄ Reception and Information office

Sick visitors

In the Accueils some 70,000 sick every year are welcomed. Voluntary helpers, doctors, nurses, hospital workers, brancardiers etc... are all there with a happy smile to offer their charitable services.

There are two Hospital reception Offices near the Grotto and there are seven others in the town itself.

◄ Helping a sick person

The Medical Bureau

A meeting place for doctors. It is here that reported cures are carefully examined. A series of showcases display a number of recognised miracles. Conferences are organised regularly (see noticeboards).

◄ Medical Bureau

The Youth at Lourdes

Lourdes is the great Meeting-place for youth from all over the world (300,000 every year). For them there are reception offices, places for various ceremonies and a very big Camp.

Youth Camp ▶

The poor at Lourdes

Everyone should be able to visit Bernadette's town, as she was a poor girl too. The Secours Catholique keeps a bureau open at the Cité Secours Saint-Pierre and it is there for this purpose.

Cité Saint Pierre - City of the Poor ▶

Day pilgrims

Every day from July 1st until September 16th a Day's pilgrimage is organised. It starts at the Statue of the Crowned Virgin at 9.00 a.m. and you will be guided, free of charge, throughout the day by priests and seminarians happy to greet you in your own language.

We wish you a happy pilgrimage.

Statue of the Crowned Virgin ▶

Silence and prayer in the Grotto

At the Grotto

Now is the time for silent prayer
« I want people to come here » said Our Lady.

The first masses of the day follow one another, in all languages in the quiet contemplation of the morning.

Here Pope John Paul II prayed in silence for a long time from the moment of his arrival in Lourdes on August 14th 1983.

Here, before the rock, we remember Bernadette's « young Lady », the Immaculate Virgin who came smiling towards the poor girl from the Cachot. It is thus that God reaches out to us, the poor beings that we are.

How good it is to pray here.

At the Crypt

The Crypt is open to all, just above the Grotto. Bernadette once prayed there. Let us admire the monstrance of the Blessed Sacrament given to Lourdes by John Paul II. In the triangle of crystal, symbolizing the Holy Trinity, the host is placed on the dried branch of a grape vine, a reminder that Christ gave his life for us.

The Crypt - with the Monstrance   ▼

The Upper Basilica

The Upper Basilica (of the Immaculate Conception) is built above the crypt ; this is the « chapel » requested by Our Lady. Evidence of the original fervour and of the first healings are to be seen engraved on the marble, while scenes of the Apparitions are depicted on the stained glass windows. Inaugurated in 1876 (visit from left to right).

Interior of the Upper Basilica ▶

The Rosary Basilica

The Rosary Basilica with its characteristic crown. As the Upper Basilica proved to be too small it was built and inaugurated in 1901. The events in the life of Christ may be seen while visiting the fifteen chapels from left to right, with the Mysteries of the Rosary depicted on large mosaics.

1 - 2 : Interior of the Rosary Basilica ▶

Crowds and Basilicas ▶

The Saint Pius X Basilica

The Saint Pius X Basilica (the Underground Basilica). Inaugurated in 1958 for the Centenary of the Apparitions. This is one of the largest Churches in the world (space for 25,000 people). Every Wednesday and Sunday at 9 a.m. (from Easter to All Saints Day) an International Mass is celebrated Here.

Interior of St Pius X Basilica ▶

The Church of Saint-Bernadette

The Church of Saint-Bernadette. More than 5 million pilgrims come to Lourdes each year. To meet the needs of this vast and still growing number of people a new Church had to be built. The Church of Saint-Bernadette built in a modern style has space for 5000 people. It has been built in the area where Bernadette came for the last Apparition.

1 - 2 : Interior of St. Bernadette's church ▶

St. Bernadette's church ▶

The Way of the Cross

The Way of the Cross comprises fifteen monumental stations, unique to Lourdes. An indispensable path to follow in order to fully grasp the message of Lourdes, the call to conversion, owing to the Passion that Jesus, Mary's son, lived out to the end for us, his brothers.

Here the water of the Grotto takes on its full meaning. It is the blood of Christ which purifies and gives life. Man is still a slave to this world of violence, hate, self-centred pleasure and weakness...

« Follow Christ and change to the side of Love » (John-Paul II).

1ˢᵗ Station

Pilate
presents the innocent
Jesus
to the leering crowd :
« Behold the man ».

2ⁿᵈ Station

Jesus receives
the Cross.
He had said :
« I lay down my life...
no one takes
it from me ».

3rd Station

Jesus falls under the
weight of the Cross.
He is not
superhuman,
he is our brother.

4th Station

Jesus meets His
Blessed Mother. Both
can say :
« Thy will be done ».

5th Station

Simon helps Jesus.
We have need
of you,
accept then our help.

6th Station

Veronica wipes
the disfigured face
of Jesus which is
the face of God.

7th Station

Jesus falls a second
time.
Greater courage is
needed to rise than
to keep from falling.

8th Station

Jesus speaks
to the women who
mourned Him :
« Do not weep for me
but rather for yourselves
and
for your children ».

9th Station

Jesus falls for the third
time.
Peter thrice denies Jesus.
Jesus asked him
the simple question
three times :
« Do you love me ? ».

10th Station

Jesus is stripped
of his clothes,
like a beggar cast out
by his own people,
he is on the side of
those that are stripped
of all.

11th Station

Jesus is nailed to the
Cross.
For all those that are
« Victims of oppression ».

12ᵗʰ Station

Death within Love.
He pardons his enemies
and the robber next to Him.
He trusts the Church and Humanity
to his mother.
He prays with the Psalms
that foretold the meaning of this day.
« My God, My God... I thirst... »,
He entrusts his life to his Father
as he has now lived his Love out
to the end
« all is accomplished ».

13th Station

Mary,
the first believer,
gathers His body up.

14th Station

Jesus is placed in
the tomb.
He went
into the entrails of
the earth
to vanquish death.

15th Station

At sunrise
on Easter day,
the stone was found ajar.
« Love is stronger
than death ».

« Drink and wash yourselves »

At the fountains

At the fountains : pray in silence ; drink a little water and wash your face. Pope John-Paul II performed these same acts.

The water of the Grotto has no magical properties. At times Almighty God has used it to perform astonishing acts of healing. It is above all the symbol of the Precious Blood and water of Christ which gushed from his pierced side to wash away our sins.

At the baths

At the baths the sick and healthy go to wash themselves (over 400,000 every year). Are they hoping for a cure ? Is it not rather to strengthen their courage ?

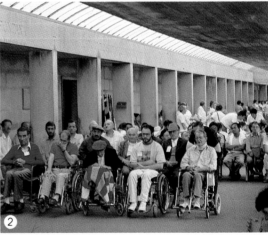

At the chapel of Reconciliation

At the chapel of Reconciliation, marked by the statue of the Priest of Ars, who dedicated his life to taking in and reconciling sinners, it is as real pilgrims that we answer Our Lady's message « Penance, Penance, Penance » (8th and 9th Apparitions).

1 : The spring   2 : Waiting to bathe
3 : The chapel of Reconciliation   ▶

The sick bathing in the pools ▶

The great moments of Lourdes

On the Esplanade

On the Esplanade most pilgrimages gather with their sick to pray near the Statue of the Crowned Virgin.

In the Meadow

In the Meadow in front of the Grotto.

It is here that the crowds gather on important occasions.

On August 15th 1983 for the **Pilgrimage of Pope John Paul II** there were 300,000 pilgrims present. This event was seen all over the world by some 800 million television viewers.

Ceremonies :
1 - 3 : On the Esplanade   2 : In the Meadow

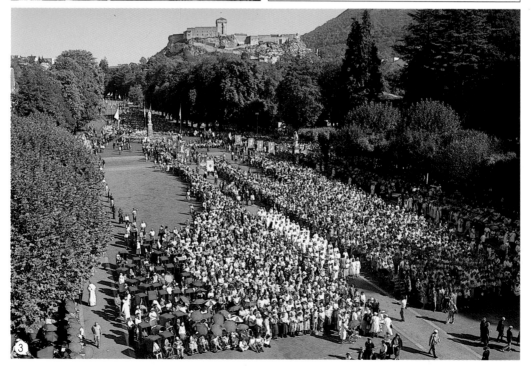

Crowds in the meadow for the occasion of the Pilgrimage of Pope John-Paul II ▶

Wonderful Procession

Every day at 4.30 p.m. there is the wonderful Procession of the Blessed Sacrament and the Blessing of the Sick.

1 - 2 - 3 - 4 - 5 - 6 : The wonderful Procession

The Grotto at night

Your candle, and those of millions of other pilgrims, will burn day and night, winter and summer. They are a witness of our faith and love before God.

In the night of this world, Lourdes keeps a light burning and keeps prayers alive.

1 - 2 - 3 : Candles at night - 4 : Assembly in front of the Grotto

Torchlight Procession

Every evening the huge Torchlight Procession starts at the Grotto and finishes at the Rosary Basilica.

Pilgrim, the « Light of Christ » has enlightened and warmed your heart during this day. Remember from now on even in the darkest night of the world, you are the « Light of Christ ». In this place all barriers fall and the joy of brotherly prayer breaks through.

We are not here to escape reality but to rediscover another reality.
The pavilions are there for meditation, discussion and meeting places for fellow pilgrims.

To see our life in the light of our faith

▲
The Catholic Action pavilion, to enlighten your life with your fellow men

Family pavilion ▶

The Handicapped pavilion, if we have been sorely tried in life
▼

▲
The Vocations pavilic if we are looking for c way in life

Senior Citizens pavili to enlighten old age
▼

The important period is « after Lourdes » when, with the Church life as a Christian awaits us.

lions

To better understand the living dynamism of the Church

e Ecumenical pavi-
n, for Christian Unity

th the Eucharistic
uth Movement ▶

e Legion of Mary,
w apostolic strength
o be found ▼

The Pax Christi pavilion,
to work towards peace
for mankind

The Missionary Pavilion
informs us of the fantas-
tic action of Christians
the world over ▼

And now, like Bernadette, let us live our lives as men, as women, as christians of today in such a way that our lives have something « to tell ».

« Go tell... » the Lady said to Bernadette. And Bernadette said : « My job is just to give you the message ; it is up to you whether you believe it or not. »